Exuberant Floral Art

natasha lisitsa

To Beth!

Enjoy exuberant Floral Art!

Love Natasha

& Scott! Love you! Carla

Jorge

Exuberant Floral Art

natasha lisitsa

stichting
kunstboek

My floral design is intuitive and my construction techniques transparent. I draw inspiration from the movement and clean lines of Ikebana, and add to this foundation a passion for exuberant colors and materials.

In this book, I wanted to take you through a visual journey of the 'essential elements' that define my design process - Materials and Texture, Color, and Movement and Space. In my work, these design elements are distinct but they overlap as well. One common thread is a sense of mischief - it's important to me that there's curiosity or wonder in each piece, whether through unconventional materials and color compositions or sheer scale.

Through our lives, we often develop inhibitions and feel like we have to color inside the lines. I try to break away from this instinct and disregard the rules. I hope this book will inspire you to break some rules too.

5

Phalaenopsis amabilis
Agapanthus africanus (dried and painted)
Salix matsudana
Licuala grandis
pheasant feather

Essential Elements

materials and texture

6 An interesting material is often the starting point for my designs. I like to forage to find inspiration, whether it's a walk on the beach that leads me to sea fans and driftwood, or a trip to the hardware store where I come across a fabulous piece of wire mesh.

I love to discover unusual and striking materials, and manipulate them to create something new and exciting.

In my view, every floral piece should have some spice – like succulents, exotic tropicals, painted branches, metals, driftwood, rattan caning, feathers, or jewels. The French might call it *jolie laide*, the beauty found in the unconventional.

While layering materials adds texture and interest, I let the different elements breathe and give them space to show their individuality.

Phalaenopsis
Aranthera
Cymbidium
Echeveria
Arctostaphylos
Gorgonia

branches

8 3-meter chandelier constructed
of painted branches, feathers,
flowers, and butterflies.

Arctostaphylos
Salix matsudana
Heliconia psittacorum
Lilium 'Sumatra'
pheasant feathers
feather butterflies

Segments of willow trunks nailed together form a sculptural framework for the lush blooms.   11

Salix matsudana
Gloriosa rothschildiana
Paeonia
Eucalyptus ficifolia (flowers)
Viburnum davidii (berries)

12 Split bamboo suspended from manzanita branches were inspired
by the poem slips that hang from a Japanese wishing tree.

Arctostaphylos
Paeoniaceae
Dahlia
Phyllostachys
Phalaenopsis
Dendrobium

13

floral curiosities

14 To create interest and
excitement, I like to use
succulents, air plants,
exotic tropicals, and
other floral curiosities.

Phalaenopsis amabilis
Cattleya
Gloriosa superba 'Rotschildiana'
Mokara
Cymbidium
Anthurium
Ixora coccinea
Rosa
Gladiolus

◄
Paphiopedilum
Clematis
Brazilia
Tillandsia
Fritillaria
Ranunculus asiaticus

►
Tillandsia
Echeveria
Passiflora
Muehlenbeckia complexa

18

▲
Paeonia
Aeonium arboreum 'Zwartkop'
Cosmos atrosanguineus
Dicranopteris linearis
Zantedeschia
Cymbidium
Eucharis grandiflora
Quercus

▶
Leucospermum nutans
Zantedeschia
Ranunculus asiaticus
Cosmos atrosanguineus
Rosa canina
Heteromeles arbutifolia
Ricinus communis

◄

Protea cynaroides
Rosa
Eustoma grandiflorum
Astilbe
Brassica oleracea
Viburnum
Hydrangea macrophylla 'Ayesha' (Popcorn)
Allium aflatunense
Erica
Rubus fruticosus

▲

Paphiopedilum
Tillandsia ionantha
Sapium sebiferum

metals

22   The polished industrial feel of metals,
along with their color and sheen, are
a striking counterpoint to natural materials.

Salix matsudana
Heliconia 'Lobster Claw'

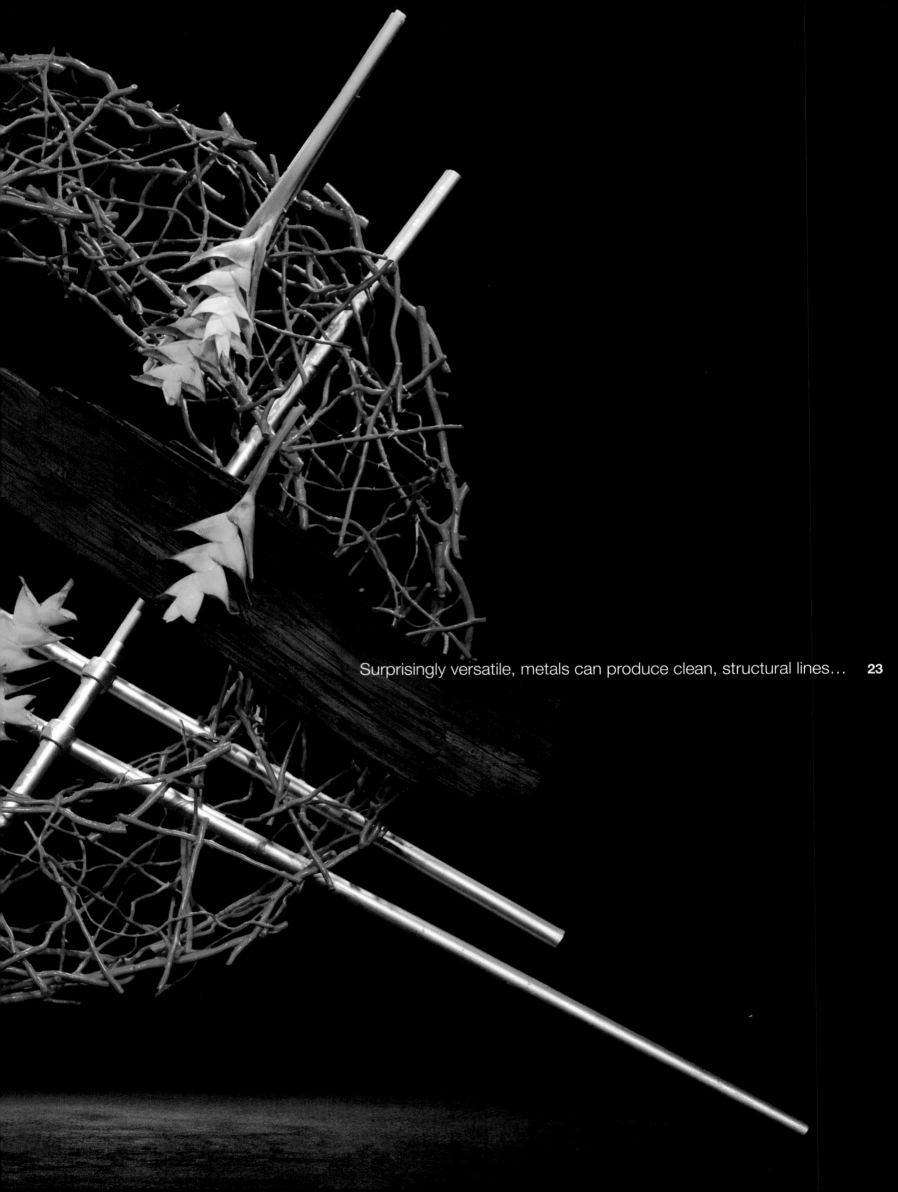

Surprisingly versatile, metals can produce clean, structural lines... **23**

24   …or be manipulated to create sensual, sweeping gestures.

Gloriosa superba 'Rotschildiana'
Zantedeschia 'Mango'

paper

26 Packaging paper, destined
for the recycling bin, can have
a rich, gruff texture that plays
well with soft flowers.

Quercus suber (bark)
Phalaenopsis
Phyllostachys
paper

palm boots and bamboo

Phyllostachys
Phoenix canariensis
Alpinia purpurata
Dianthus
Craspedia globosa
Strelitzia reginae

30

Phyllostachys
Phoenix canariensis
Alpinia purpurata
Dianthus
Craspedia globosa
Strelitzia reginae

Zantedeschia 'Mango'
Clematis
Tulipa 'Dordogne'
Mokara
Vanda
rattan caning

rattan caning

earth in play

Elements of Nature series.
1000 meters of rattan caning
twisted into spirals represents
crowns of trees in a harmonious
ecosystem. There is a sense of
joy in the playful composition.

Salix matsudana
Corylus avellana
Agapanthus orientalis
Anthurium andraenum 'Apple Green'
rattan caning

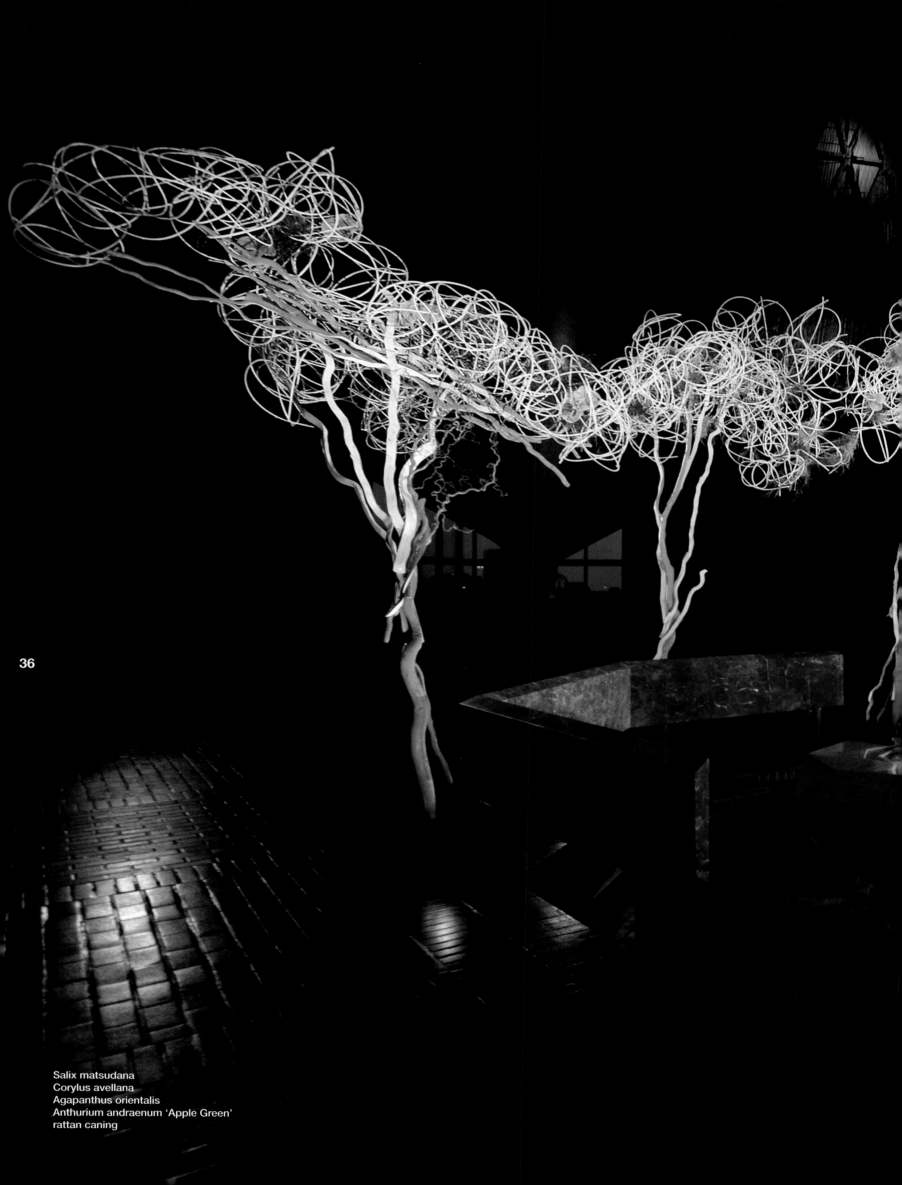

36

Salix matsudana
Corylus avellana
Agapanthus orientalis
Anthurium andraenum 'Apple Green'
rattan caning

driftwood

38 Driftwood sculpture with metal, acrylic, feathers, and plants was inspired by a ballerina in motion.

Corylus avellana
Phalaenopsis
Kalanchoe luciae
pheasant feathers
metal stripping
driftwood

40 Rustic, gnarly driftwood is a nice canvas for a burst of color.

feathers

Paphiopedilum
Zantedeschia `Majestic Red´
Oncidium `Chocolate´
Amaryllis
Passiflora
Cibotium menziesii `Hapu'u´
Gloriosa Rothschildiana
peacock feathers
pheasant feathers

jewels

Jewelry design in collaboration with Masha Avina

Hydrangea
Anemone
Zantedeschia
Brunia silver
Tulipa (fringed)
Allium sphaerocephalon
peacock feather

tree barks

Quercus suber (bark)
Leucospermum bolusii

48

Quercus suber (bark)
Ranunculus asiaticus
Zantedeschia
Leucospermum bolusii
Larix decidua (cone)

floating on air

Elements of Nature series.
The installation envelops
the baptismal font with a blanket
of swaying pampas grass.
Wind-like swirls of brass wire
and delicate leaves
and flowers hover above.

Cortaderia selloana
Lunaria annua
Physalis alkekengi

52

Cortaderia selloana
Lunaria annua
Physalis alkekengi

Essential Elements

color

54 Color evokes mood and stimulates the senses. I love to generate excitement, and it's fun and subversive to create a visual shock wave with vibrant colors and startling color combinations.

Gloriosa superba 'Rotschildiana'
Leucospermum gerrardii
Phoenix dactylifera
Citrus mandarine
Arctostaphylos

56

Gloriosa superba 'Rotschildiana'
Leucospermum nutans
Leucospermum gerrardii
Guzmania (Bromelia)
Ranuculus asiaticus
Tulipa peony
Licuala grandis
decorative wires

58

▲
Dahlia hortensis
Phalaenopsis amabilis
Gloriosa superba 'Rotschildiana'
Celosia cristata
Rosa

▶
Phalaenopsis amabilis
Agapanthus africanus (dried and painted)
Salix matsudana
Paeonia
Gloriosa superba 'Rotschildiana'
Gorgonia
Licuala grandis
pheasant feather

▲
Paeonia 'Red Charm'
Zantedeschia
Leucospermum nutans
Ranunculus asiaticus
Gloriosa superba 'Rotschildiana'
Oncidium flexuosum
Rosa 'Graham Thomas'

▶
Paeonia 'Red Charm'
Zantedeschia
Leucospermum nutans
Ranunculus asiaticus
Gloriosa superba 'Rotschildiana'
Oncidium flexuosum
Rosa 'Graham Thomas'

63

▲
Paphiopdeilum
Zantedeschia
Leucospermum nutans
Aranthera
Eryngium planum
Anemone
Gloriosa Rothschildiana

▶
Phalaenopsis amabilis
Zantedeschia
Cymbidium
Miltonia
Morus alba 'Unryu'
Rosa Canina

66

68

Rosa
Gypsophila 'Million Stars'

69

▼
Tulipa
Tulipa 'Canary'
Papaver nudicaule
Mokara
Ornithogalum dubium
Citrus sinensis
Citrus limon
Citrus aurantifolia

▶
Tulipa
Tulipa 'Canary'
Papaver nudicaule
Leucospermum nutans
Craspedia
Citrus japonica

monochrome

70 A powerful effect can be created
by using monochromatic color
– which allows the textural or
structural elements of the design
to shine.

Monochromatic white creates an elegant feel amid the rustic wood in an old barn.

Arctostaphylos
Phalaenopsis amabilis
Dendrobium

73

Designed In collaboration with Mary Podgurski

movement and space

74 To create dynamic movement, I like to play with gesture and space. I compose materials in relation to both the physical space surrounding the design, and the negative space formed by the design itself.

Phyllostachys
Heliconia psittacorum
Heliconia caribaea

through the fire

Elements of Nature series.
Inspired by fire, a flame-shaped
structure flares upward over
the central aisle of the cathedral.
Fifty triangles made of 500 meters
of bamboo interlock to form
a 10-meter tall curvature, creating a
sensation of movement and tension.

Phyllostachys
Heliconia psittacorum
Heliconia carribaea

Phyllostachys
Heliconia psittacorum
Heliconia carribaea

78

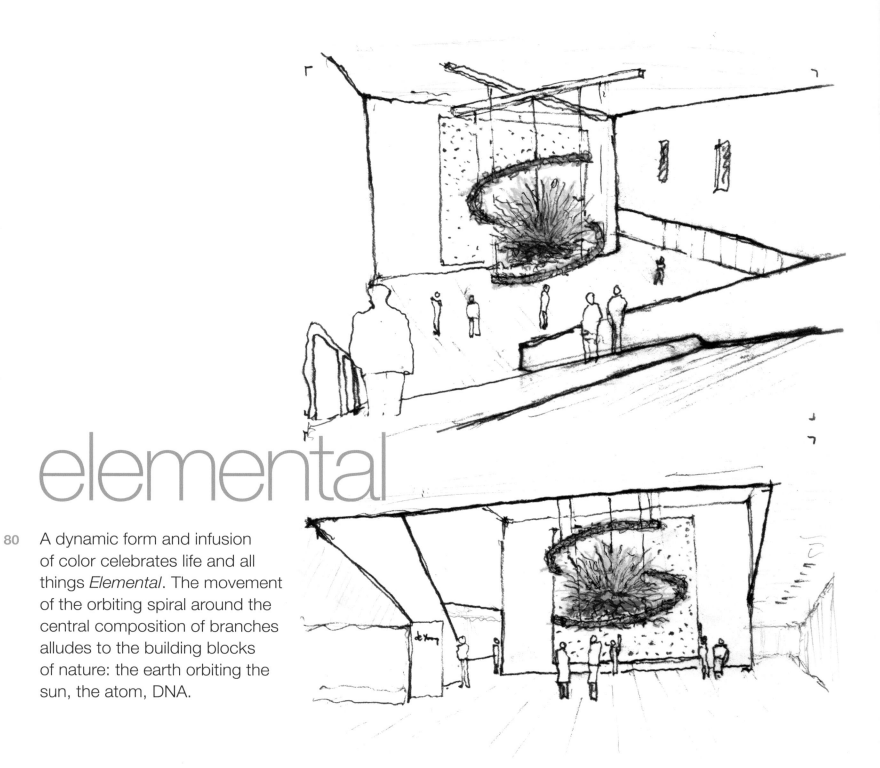

elemental

A dynamic form and infusion of color celebrates life and all things *Elemental*. The movement of the orbiting spiral around the central composition of branches alludes to the building blocks of nature: the earth orbiting the sun, the atom, DNA.

Forsythia x intermedia
Arctostaphylos
Salix matsudana
Anthurium

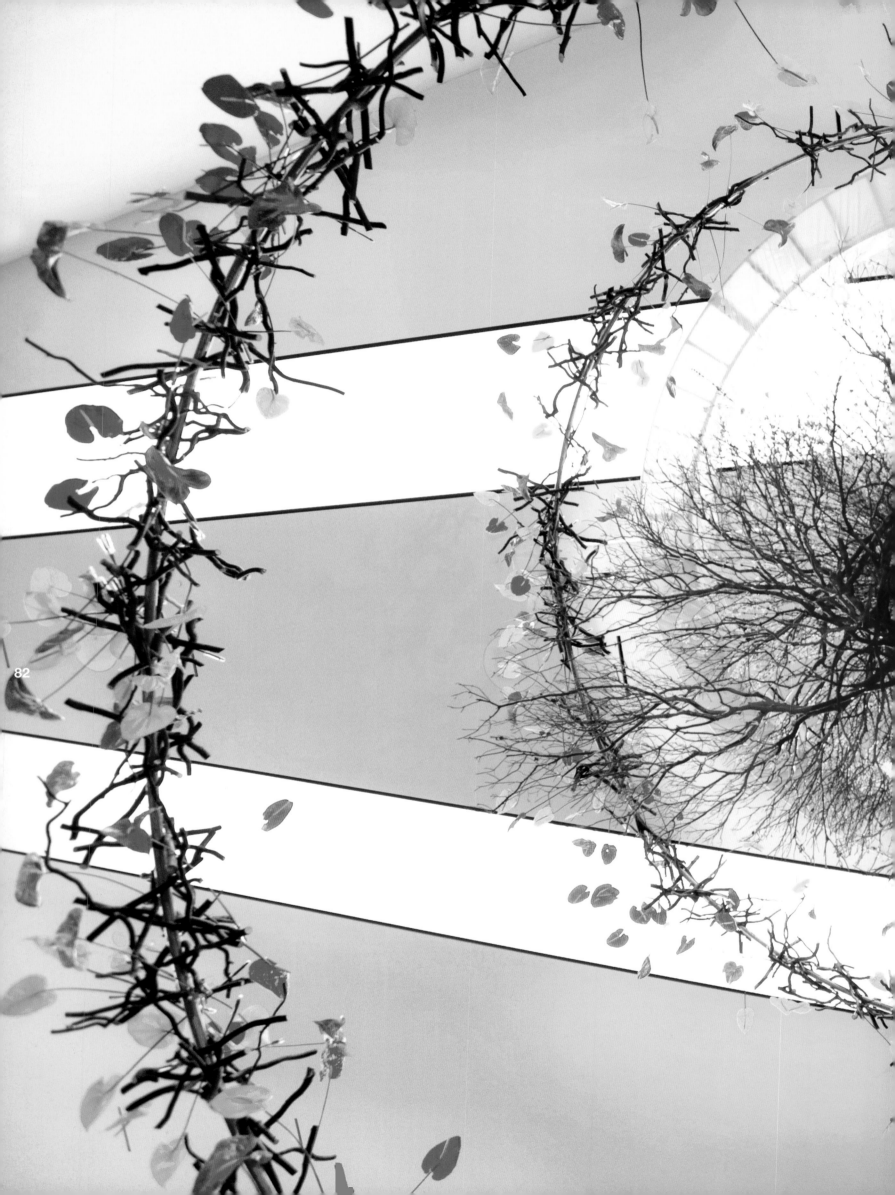

Forsythia x intermedia
Arctostaphylos
Salix matsudana
Anthurium

84

Forsythia x intermedia
Arctostaphylos
Salix matsudana
Anthurium

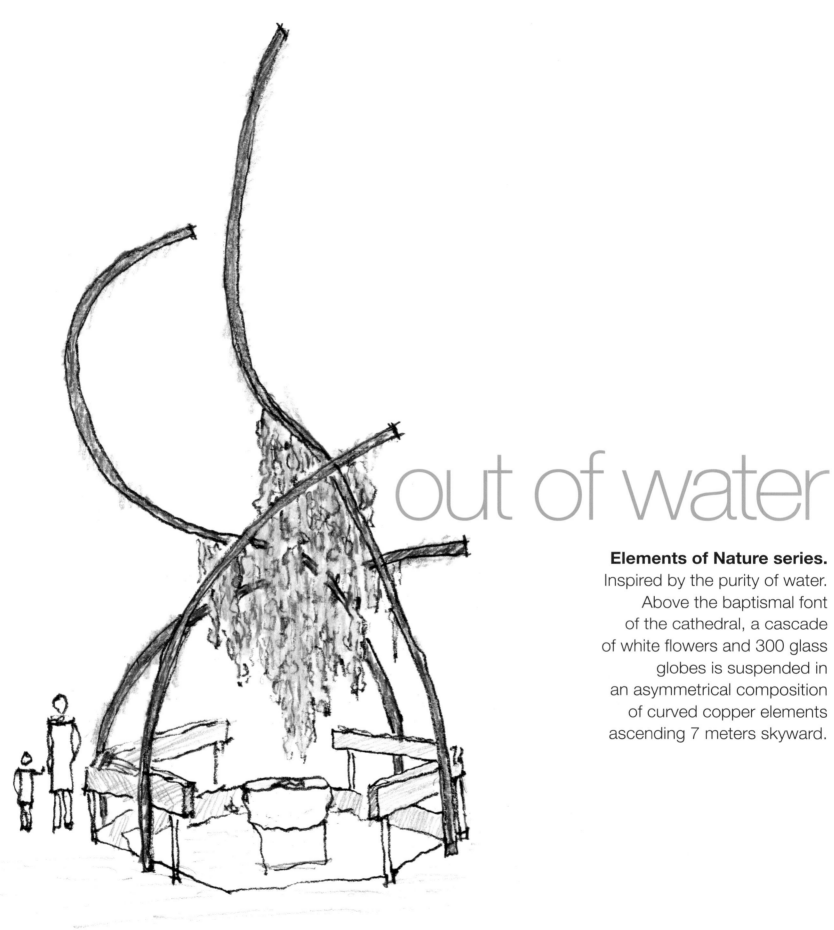

out of water

Elements of Nature series.
Inspired by the purity of water.
Above the baptismal font
of the cathedral, a cascade
of white flowers and 300 glass
globes is suspended in
an asymmetrical composition
of curved copper elements
ascending 7 meters skyward.

Morus alba `Unryu´
Phalaenopsis
Dendrobium

Morus alba `Unryu´
Phalaenopsis
Dendrobium

90 Curly willow trunks sawn in half evoke the sensual pose of the Venus statue...

Gloriosa superba 'Rotschildiana'
Phalaenopsis
Zantedeschia `Schwarzwalder´
Salix matsudana

92   ...their movement mirrored in a delicate, and ultimately harmonious, balance.

Salix matsudana
Craspedia globosa

about natasha and waterlily pond

94 **Natasha Lisitsa**, owner and lead designer of Waterlily Pond Floral and Event Design Studio in San Francisco, USA, has become internationally recognized for her vivacious style and innovative use of materials. Natasha worked as an engineer before leaving the high-tech industry to pursue her love of flowers and design. She studied at the Sogetsu School of Ikebana and developed her own style fusing Eastern and Western principles, often referred to as 'exuberant Ikebana'.

Natasha founded Waterlily Pond Studio in 2001 and grew it into one of the most sought-after sources for floral art and event design in the San Francisco Bay Area and beyond. Waterlily Pond has created flowers and decor for over 1000 weddings and special events.

The studio has been commissioned by the San Francisco Museum of Modern Art, the de Young Museum and other prominent cultural organizations to create large-scale floral art installations, some of them up to 500 kilograms (1000 pounds) in weight.

Natasha loves to share her passion for exuberant floral art with other designers and enthusiasts in lecture-demonstrations.

She represented the USA in the international wedding design book Florever Wherever, featuring designers from across the world, published by Stichting Kunstboek. Her work has been featured in many international and U.S. publications.

Dedication

Many of the designs in this book have been created in collaboration with my design team – my amazing husband Daniel Schultz, also an architect and furniture designer, and my right hand and dear friend Carla Parkinson, a talented floral designer and Ikebana enthusiast. Working with my team on the progression of a design, from conception to realization, is a true joy and allows my designs to soar.

Acknowledgements

My family for their unconditional love and support.
My daughter Dana Roytenberg for help with conceptualization of this book.
Erin Beach of Erin Beach Photography for a huge contribution to this book and always having her camera at the ready.
Judy Parker of Gertrude and Mabel Photography for capturing many of the designs through a series of photoshoots.
Alison Bradley for encouragement and guidance.
All of the talented photographers whose work is featured here.

Cover
Gloriosa superba 'Rotschildiana'
Morus alba `Unryu´
Agapanthus

Page 2
Arctostaphylos
Phyllostachys
Rosa
Cymbidium
Phalaenopsis
Paeoniaceae
Dendrobium
Aranthera

Text and Arrangements
Natasha Lisitsa
www.waterlilypond.com

Photography
Anna Kuperberg
Arrowood Photography
Cliff Brunk Photography
Dekker Photography
Della Chen Photo
Erin Beach Photography
Gertrude and Mabel Photography
Larissa Cleveland Photography
Sara Allen, Onelove Photography
Jocelyn Knight Photography
Kim and Nicky Photography
Orange Photography
Pictilio Photography
Rachel Thurston

Lay-out
Group Van Damme
www.groupvandamme.eu

Print
PurePrint
www.pureprint.be

Final Editing
Katrien Van Moerbeke

Published by
Stichting Kunstboek bvba
Legeweg 165
B-8020 Oostkamp
Belgium
Tel. +32 50 46 19 10
Fax +32 50 46 19 18
info@stichtingkunstboek.com
www.stichtingkunstboek.com

ISBN 978-90-5856-394-1
D/2013/6407/1
NUR 421